Nft for Beginners

Learn the Basics of Investing in Digital Crypto Art
and Collectibles to Make a Profit
(2022 Guide for Newbies)

Shaun Badman

TABLE OF CONTENTS

CHAPTER 1: NFT (NON-FUNGIBLE TOKEN)

NFTs (non-fungible tokens) are popular and will remain so for some time. It's being discussed not only in cryptocurrency circles, but also in the press, on social media, and beyond!

It's a buzzword that has everyone wondering what it is and how it works. Most importantly, how they may benefit from it.

NFTs are a notion that might be perplexing to many people, especially those who are unfamiliar with cryptocurrencies. But once you've grasped it, your mind will be blown by how incredible this opportunity is and how vital it is for you to be a part of it.

Crypto art is a ten-year-old notion that was previously only available to early cryptocurrency users and investors. It was like insider information, to be shared and celebrated with like-minded people hoping for cryptocurrencies to transform the world.

But all of that is about to change. Since the cryptocurrency explosion, with Bitcoin at the forefront and showing no signs of abating anytime soon, the technology has grown, with NFTs taking center stage.

The COVID-19 pandemic aided with this; because many people worldwide were unable to leave their homes, they found themselves with extra money to spend, which they did: online. In a moment of uncertainty, the worldwide populace turned to technology for pleasure and solace.

With so many people online, a slew of bitcoin businesses based on NFTs have sprung up, with more on the way. Over $250 million in NFTs were traded in 2020, a 299 percent increase over the previous year, and this figure is expected to rise much further (Iredale, 2021). Everyone wants to be a part of it, from celebrities to local artists to everyone trying to make money through trading.

This is where you come in, and why it's critical to understand everything there is to know about NFTs before embarking on your trading path. This is a beginner's tutorial, but it will also be valuable for people who are already familiar with bitcoin and want to break into this new and exciting venture. It is crucial to understand that I am not a financial advisor and am not licensed to provide financial advice. This is simply a guide based on data received. My book covers the fundamentals of cryptocurrencies and Bitcoin, so no matter how much you already know, you'll have all you need to understand how it all works. The fundamentals of cryptocurrencies, as well as the concepts that will be repeated throughout the book, are critical.

It may appear perplexing at first, but I assure you that the material will stick with you and will help you master NFTs with ease. Now is the moment to learn more and become a part of history while also earning money!

CHAPTER 2: CRYPTOCURRENCY

Modern cryptocurrency has existed since 2009 when Bitcoin was first made available to the general public. There are significantly more cryptocurrencies available now, not just Bitcoin, in 2021. The world of cryptocurrency is bigger than ever, with new countries joining all the time and various marketplaces for people to use all across the world.

Cryptocurrency has demonstrated that it is not just for technology enthusiasts or those looking to change the way the financial system works, but that anybody can and should be a part of it. Cryptocurrency is here to stay, as are technological breakthroughs, the most recent of which being NFTs. To really comprehend NFTs, you must first grasp their history, which begins with the history of Bitcoin.

THE EVOLUTION OF CRYPTOCURRENCY

The majority of cryptocurrencies today are variants of Bitcoin, the first extensively utilized cryptocurrency. It was founded in 2009 by Satoshi Nakamoto, a programmer, to usher in a new technological era of blockchain and decentralized digital currencies.

That may sound like a mouthful, but it will be explained shortly.

Satoshi Nakamoto is a pseudonym, as it is uncertain who they are or if they exist at all. It is speculated that Satoshi Nakamoto is the pseudonym used by the Bitcoin creators, hence Satoshi Nakamoto could be a group of people rather than a single person. They would be a millionaire now if they were just one person. Bitcoin started with a whitepaper, which is a document that gives concise information on the topic at hand. The Bitcoin whitepaper, which was published in 2008, was revolutionary. Bitcoin was the first publicly recognized cryptocurrency, but others predated it and influenced its development.

CARD READERS

One of the first attempts was done in the 1980s in the Netherlands, with the development of smart cards for petrol stations that were prone to midnight thefts. This was a major issue because gas stations had to stay open overnight in order for trucks to refuel. A group of developers collaborated to attach money to smart cards for the drivers to utilize. Truck drivers used the cards to pay, thus the gas stations didn't save any cash and couldn't be robbed.

FLOOZ

Flooze.com began employing e-currency as part of its marketing strategy in 1998. You may purchase one Flooz for $1 and spend it on the company's website. This cash could be used on other websites as well. Stores who participated received bonuses, which encouraged other stores to participate in their promotion. It cost $1 million to market, and Whoopi Goldberg served as their spokesman. The premise was strong enough and popular enough that it raised $35 million in venture money (Rossen, 2017).

Unfortunately, it was not sustainable and resulted in significant financial losses for the organization. Because not all of the retailers participated, the corporation struck a deal with the vendors to guarantee its transactions, whether they were fraudulent or not. This resulted in Russian and Philippine hackers utilizing stolen credit cards to make purchases on the Flooze.com site, which drew the attention of the FBI. It was not safe and secure, leaving it vulnerable to scammers, who debilitated it to the point of closure. Many of the concepts utilized in cryptocurrency today are based on that failed initiative, which had great promise but awful timing.

DIGICASH

David Chaum, an American cryptographer, devised the idea of a token that could be safely passed between individuals and replaced currency. It was encrypted using a 'blinding formula' or Blind Signature Technology, which he presented in a scholarly article in 1983. That is, the token would have an authentication signature and could be updated without being traceable, even by banks or governments.

Chaum founded Digicash in 1989 so that he could employ this technique, but it did not work, and the company went bankrupt in 1998. It appeared too complicated, and investors were hesitant to back something so dangerous, especially since e-commerce was unfamiliar to them at the time. That doesn't mean it was all in vain, as many of the Digicash principles, formulas, and encryption technologies were used in the construction of the present digital currency.

B-MONEY

Wei Dai, a developer, also proposed an anonymous, distributed electronic cash system dubbed B-money in 1998. Dai proposed using two distinct protocols, resulting in a structure that is quite different from Bitcoin. B-money stood for the same thing as Bitcoin: a safe, private means for transferring money across a decentralized network without the assistance of a third party.

Despite the whitepaper, B-money did not take off since investors were not willing to take a bet on such a thing and it was not exciting enough for people to pay attention to at the time. To his credit, Wei Dan's B-money was mentioned in the Bitcoin whitepaper because of the impact it had on the establishment of Bitcoin.

PAYPAL

Many firms arose in the 1990s, and many of them were founded on a similar idea to Digicash. PayPal was the most popular, and it is still in use today. It was one of the first to allow for online payments, allowing individuals to transfer money rapidly and securely through computer browsers.

PayPal subsequently linked up with eBay, which was a wise decision because it expanded not only its user base but also the firm itself. That is why it remains popular. PayPal is backed by countries all over the world and is a popular platform for freelancers to be paid for their work. PayPal has become so commonplace that it's hard to believe that it was innovative just a few decades ago!

E-GOLD

E-gold, which was inspired by PayPal's web base technology, dealt with the online gold trade before expanding to cover worthless silver and other precious metals. Users of the platform were given online credit in exchange for these products. It was very popular, especially because no onshore approval was required in the United States.

E-gold, which was launched in 1996, was likewise insufficiently secure, and its popularity drew organized criminal syndicates that utilized malware and phishing scams to target the corporation. Things deteriorated to the point where the federal government of the United States had to shut it down in 2005.

BITGOLD

Despite the fact that it has a similar name to gold, BitGold did not deal with gold exchange. Its name derives from the need for the money to be backed by genuine gold. It was a step toward decentralizing currency. Nick Szabo developed the concept about the same time as B-money in 1998.

This computer scientist, legal scholar, and cryptographer created BitGold to involve machines in solving cryptographic riddles: that is, exceedingly complicated puzzles that a human cannot solve. The solved riddles would be stored in a safe encrypted registry, and the solver would be given a public key. Then, a new puzzle would begin based on the previous solve, forming a chain. Today, crypto-mining is based on this method.

Despite the fact that it is only a concept, BitGold has served as the foundation for many of the digital currencies that are available today. Many have worked out the kinks and built their currencies around BitGold.

HASH MONEY

This piece of software was built in 1997 by Adam Black, a British cryptographer and cypherpunk (someone who advocates for privacy and encryption for a political change).

The goal of Hash Cash was to use a proof-of-work method to prevent spam emails and denial of service assaults. This means that one party must prove that the computer's work is correct, which is accomplished through a lot of backend code requiring cryptography. So, once again, computers solve tough puzzles: a pattern develops.

This software is still available. Of fact, it is employed as part of the mining system in cryptocurrency, namely Bitcoin. Mining will be covered later in this chapter.

WHAT EXACTLY IS BLOCKCHAIN?

A blockchain database is a sort of database. That is, it is a structured collection of information that can be accessed by a computer system and is quite exact in how it saves its data. Consider a storage warehouse for information that is well-organized and has a unique layout from other storage warehouses.

Blockchains are regarded as secure databases since data cannot be changed, destroyed, or replaced. New data is recorded in a new block, which is then chained onto the following block in chronological order: thus the name blockchain. Each block carries a timestamp, allowing it to be read in chronological sequence.

Ledgers for transactions are the most prevalent sort of information maintained. Consider virtual ledgers or books that contain transactions. Other sorts of data can also be saved on the blockchain; it all depends on how the software is used. Bitcoin is decentralized, which means that all users, not just a single person or organization, have control. This renders the data irreversible, ensuring that transactions are permanently logged and that any user can securely see them without anything being changed fraudulently.

All organizations rely on information, which is the data that must be saved in a database. But it must not just be stored; it must also be completed as quickly and correctly as possible, with no changes made in the process. Businesses may use blockchain to track orders, production lines, and even verify for evidence of identity quickly and efficiently.

Scammers find it difficult to defraud the system since it is so secure that ownership cannot be altered, just tracked. Furthermore, there are no third parties engaged who could alter data as it travels from one user to the next.

Blockchain technology is employed by a wide range of businesses, not simply cryptocurrencies like Bitcoin. Because it is a secure database, it has various applications that companies all around the world are interested in. Technology is no longer risky and experimental, and as it evolves, so does technology as a whole.

Large corporations do not want to be left behind, thus they have entire departments dedicated solely to blockchain technology.

IBM

With IBM Food Trust, IBM uses blockchain to track how food goods arrive at its locations. This application was developed in response to the huge number of diseases and harmful materials introduced into foods after they left the warehouse.

Having to reject infected food was costing businesses a lot of money, as well as the faith of the impacted consumers. Instead of waiting weeks to figure out what went wrong, IBM can now track food distribution in real-time. Blockchain technology has aided in food safety and consumer safety.

Blockchain technology was utilized to track data from IoT devices throughout the food's journey in order to discover where things were going wrong. IoT stands for 'internet of things,' and it simply refers to devices that contain technology that allows them to share data, such as security systems or sensors. The application has grown in

SHELL

Blockchain is being used as a platform for crude oil trade and settlement. Shell is abandoning traditional paper contracts in favor of a smart, digital, and secure system built on the VAKT blockchain platform. It also employs Komgo SA to facilitate joint commercial agreements.

Shell has established a team named Shell's Blockchain Centre of Intelligence, whose mission, in addition to the ones described above, is to collaborate with other Shell businesses to embrace blockchain technology and build on the tools and capabilities they already have.

AMAZON WEB SERVICES (AWS)

Blockchain solutions are available as software packages for businesses that do not want or cannot construct their own. There are numerous software blockchain packages available to meet specific business demands, and they can be acquired as part of a subscription with technical customer support. This is done through Amazon's AWS (Amazon Web Services) Marketplace, so businesses can choose from a variety of solutions or contact the corporation for assistance in navigating them.

ANTHEM

Since 2019, this health insurance organization has started utilizing blockchain. They use it to provide patients with safe online access to and share their medical data. Users can use the app on their smartphones to scan the QR code and authorize access to their health records to a variety of healthcare providers.

It is currently in its early stages, so just a few people are utilizing it, but the business believes that by three years, all of its 40 million members will have access to this function. Anthem intends to employ the technology for more than a dozen new projects once it is fully launched and in use.

BMW

BMW, along with Honda and Ford, is a member of the Mobile Open Blockchain Initiative (MOBI). This implies that the auto industry will be able to begin providing new cars with a digital identity in July 2019 through its blockchain vehicle identity standard. It is projected that in the future, technology will be able to track the life of the car and share data. This data could be utilized to improve automobiles.

MOBI is committed to using blockchain technology to make mobility services more environmentally friendly. By collaborating with companies and governments as well as car manufacturers, we can make transportation more inexpensive, less congested, and safer. BMW is running a test initiative with suppliers in Europe and the United States to follow materials, components, and parts across the supply chain on its own. PartChain is the name of the system, and it is being rolled out to more suppliers.

GE (GENERAL ELECTRIC)

General Electric has created a 'back-to-birth' record for an airplane engine through its Aviation business. This record contains information on the manufacturing process as well as the maintenance that was done. It prevents engines from being used if the paperwork is incomplete, which is a major concern in the sector. There is now a computerized paper trail for these parts, allowing trade to continue.

Since its inception, the company has made significant investments in blockchain technologies in order to propel its business forward.

JP MORGAN & CO.

Blockchain is used by one of America's largest banks. Cross-border transfers that used to take up to two weeks are now completed in minutes thanks to its Interbank Information Network.

It is known as Confirm, and it is expected to reduce rejected or returned transactions due to payment information, lowering expenses for both sending and receiving institutions. Before anything is processed, the information is double-checked, reducing errors and allowing payments to be completed more quickly.

According to JP Morgan, 100 institutions use this blockchain via a common ledger, which explains why delays are cleared so rapidly.

NASDAQ

NASDAQ was an early adopter of blockchain, using it since 2015 and releasing a slew of goods. In 2017, a significant product was an electronic voting tool for South Africa's central securities depository. This meant that voters could vote remotely and safely via an app. It is also expanding into new areas and is far ahead of the competition with its blockchain solutions.

SAMSUNG

Nexledger Universal was designed so that anyone who wished to execute agreements may easily and quickly prove their identities. It is now used by 18 Korean banks through the

BankSign application. People use this software to allow banks to identify them even when they are not visiting their own bank. It is so popular that 235,000 individuals have already signed up for it (del Castillo, 2021).

Nexledger Universal is also being used by the Samsung Group to verify patient identities in order to expedite health insurance claims, among other things.

THE UNITED NATIONS

This demonstrates that blockchain technology may help any firm. The United Nations has around 193 members and uses several blockchain applications to manage them.

One is used to provide funds to people who have been displaced by war. To prevent warlords from taking these monies, they used blockchain-verified iris scans rather than ID cards.

The United Nations now has five blockchain initiatives in the works through their United Nations Innovation Network.

BLOCKCHAIN'S DISADVANTAGES

Based on how quickly the technology has developed and continues to grow, the benefits of using blockchain are numerous and exciting. However, in order to have an open mind, it is necessary to be aware of some of the disadvantages and concerns.

It will take some time to smooth out all of the kinks, but with so many enterprises developing their own platforms, some of these issues should not be a deterrent.

COST

Because the technology costs so much, not to mention the implementation costs, it is not yet feasible for smaller enterprises to begin adopting blockchain. However, with so many large corporations establishing departments and teams solely for blockchain technology, it should help offset many of the costs in the future.

ILLEGAL ACTIVITIES

There is a history of illegal activity, although it was only 2.1 percent in 2019, and it is expected to shrink to 0.34 percent in 2020. (Lennon, 2021). It is unrealistic to believe that criminals would not take advantage of any chance for their commercial activities, but that does not mean that the blockchain is only their realm.

GLOBAL GOVERNANCE

Blockchain is unregulated, and its decentralized nature has many countries concerned about its stability. China, Russia, and Columbia have all banned Bitcoin and the thousands of other cryptocurrencies that are now available.

The United States, on the other hand, has not imposed a prohibition, and the federal government has left it up to the various states to adopt their own norms and regulations. In 2015, New York became the first state to begin regulating cryptocurrencies, with 32 states following suit with a few regulations already in place. Europe only began regulating in 2020 and largely adheres to the United States' approach of 'to each their own.'

This has generated a lot of gray areas in global regulation, which is problematic but not enough to prevent the technology from being implemented globally.

SELF-MAINTENANCE

Users control their own blockchain wallets, which might lead to data loss if you're not careful. If you forget your password and are unable to restore it, your data is lost.

The same is true for your cryptocurrency wallet: if you lose your key or log-in credentials, you lose everything, which could be thousands of dollars depending on how far you've progressed with usage. The same criteria apply to online safety, which is to keep sensitive information secure and off the internet. Most importantly, practice utilizing two-factor authentication: an electronic mechanism for gaining access to a website only after two methods are offered and entered. There are numerous apps to pick from, all of which are simple to use.

WHY DO WE NOW USE CRYPTOCURRENCIES?

Cryptocurrency is used to buy and sell products just like any other currency, and as its popularity grows, more corporations are joining in, and for good reason. At the time of writing, these are a few places where crypto is being employed.

MONEY TRANSFERS AT LOW COST

This simply means that while buying and selling through transactions, you obtain what you desire in less time. When it comes to international money transfers, it is also cheaper because there are no third parties involved, such as banks. So, if you want to buy a couch from a furniture store, you pay the listed amount. There are no bank or transaction fees to worry about.

TRAVEL

Certain travel agencies now accept cryptocurrency as payment for flights, car rentals, and hotel accommodations. When traveling, you can also convert cryptocurrencies so that you have the local currency on hand.

With over 2,500 cryptocurrencies accessible now that are used globally, the tourism sector couldn't afford to miss out on this significant potential. As travelers develop, so must the business in order to keep up.

You can also pay for your space flight with Virgin Galactic using Bitcoin.

INVESTMENTS IN STARTUPS

Previously, only the affluent and large corporations could invest in startups, but the world has changed dramatically. You may now invest in the startups you want to see succeed as long as you have enough money in your cryptocurrency wallet.

Most entrepreneurs are ecstatic about this since it ensures that they will be able to obtain sufficient money without the assistance of large investors. This has permitted the formation of various enterprises financed by their fans, as well as a shift in how people invest in businesses.

The most significant distinction is that the enterprises are not certain to succeed, and these new investors are aware of this. They do it because it is part of the process of investing in and growing the sector, and it is extremely revolutionary.

CRYPTOCURRENCY MINING

This began with Bitcoin mining, in which anyone could mine for Bitcoin using their personal computers. These machines solved complex mathematical equations in exchange for a proportion of Bitcoin.

Because of the complexity of today's Bitcoin mining installations, it no longer generates as much passive money as it did ten years ago. Fortunately, more cryptocurrencies allow for passive revenue generation through mining. The most popular are Ethereum and NiceHash.

ETHEREUM

To mine Ethereum, all you need is a graphics card with at than 4 gigabytes of video RAM, which you can get from any computer store, an Ethereum wallet by signing up, and, of course, your computer. Then, join a mining pool, such as Ethermine, since your profit as transactions is solved, something you cannot do on your own. After that, install the software and begin mining.

NICEHASH

This is a simple mining platform for beginners, which is why it is so popular. NiceHash is a mobile app that assists you in locating mining software and a pool to join. It also pays in Bitcoin, despite the fact that you're mining for Ethereum, and has slightly higher usage fees.

PAYMENT FOR CONTENT

There are a few businesses that will pay for content with cryptocurrency. It all started with a SteemIt, which allows you to make money in two ways: by creating original content or by interacting with posts through comments and upvotes.

There is also blogging, editing, and translation material work available on a variety of sites for a variety of cryptocurrencies. It's a fantastically inventive method to recognize and reward industry content writers.

WHY SHOULD YOU USE CRYPTOCURRENCY?

What are the benefits of using cryptocurrency? It is not as volatile as many people believe and is a very viable option to trade online.

Companies are not scared to diversify their portfolios and adapt to the changing times since it is not a passing fad; it is here to stay and is altering the internet world for the better. Online payment systems have been around for a long time, but cryptocurrency is more secure and traceable. Of course, there is also the financial guarantee that NFT trading will provide you with a substantial passive income. As a result, it is secure because all transactions are recorded on the ledger and are traceable. Because it is decentralized, it is not controlled by any government or bank, which reduces the chance of identity theft until your credentials are compromised. With so many companies joining on board, it is easily accessible, and you own it because there is no cash system through which your bitcoin must transit.

CHAPTER 2: FRACTIONAL OWNERSHIP

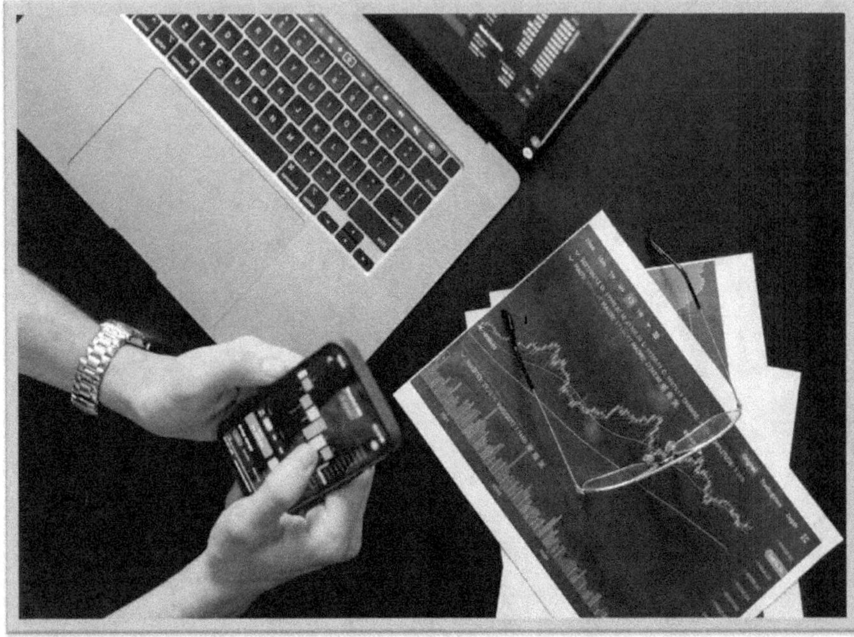

Before going into NFT investments, it is critical to understand the concept of fractional ownership. When you begin trading, you will have a clearer idea of who owns what. Although fractional ownership may appear to be a confusing newfangled concept, it has been around for quite some time. A high-value property or asset that may be utilized as a vacation house can be purchased by more than one person and the usage is shared.

Assume there are four owners in the case of the vacation home. They would split the time spent at the vacation property and the costs of maintenance and upkeep. Rent would also be divided among the owners. This allows you to own something valuable without breaking the bank, especially because you won't be utilizing it all of the time. It is appropriate in areas where there are laws in place that provide rewards for ownership.

Fractional ownership first appeared in Europe in the late 1970s under the label 'co-ownership.' It was popular in southern France, Spain, Portugal, and the Canary Islands, giving rise to the variant titles *"co-propriete," "co-propiedad," and "pro-indiviso."*

Because the utilization plans were complex and rigid, they did not last. However, it made a reappearance in the 1990s and was seen in the United States. More people desired second houses in regions recognized for their excellent skiing. Many individuals leaped on the concept because these locations were not affordable to a single person and reservation technology had advanced substantially since the 1970s. It became so popular that assets began to include jet aircraft, luxury boats, classic and supercars, artwork, and other objects.

Over the years, the sector has developed and spread throughout the world, particularly in Southeast Asia (Bali and Thailand). Things only slowed in 2008 as a result of the global financial crisis, and they have since slowed more. Despite the reduction in growth, the sector has not ceased. It is expected to accelerate as the global real estate market improves.

Even though the terms *"fractional ownership"* and "timesharing" are sometimes used interchangeably, they are not the same thing. Because of this uncertainty, the fractional ownership business needed to rebrand in order to stand out. It differs in that the owners own a portion of the real estate rather than just a time period in which they can utilize it.

A property management business is usually in charge of the property's care and maintenance, while the owners only pay the bills. So it's part ownership of something with numerous people, not renting out the use of something.

OTHER APPLICATIONS

The concept of fractional ownership was originally applied to real estate, but it has now been extended to other items.

AIRCRAFT

Individuals or businesses can purchase a share of an aircraft ranging from one-sixteenth to half. It all depends on how frequently the owner wishes to use the plane and how much they are willing to pay for that use. They must also cover a percentage of the aircraft's purchase price for the duration of the contract. This form of acquisition differs from real estate in that contracts are only valid for 5 years at most.

All additional administrative fees must also be paid and divided among the owners, with each owner promised a set amount of hours on short notice. This is possible because fractional aircraft buyers are not allotted a specific aircraft but instead have access to a pool of comparable makes and types. So, in fact, you own a share of the aviation firm and have the right to use any aircraft in the fleet under the terms of the purchase title or deed.

BUSINESS AVIATION: JET PLANES

Richard Santulli, an American businessman, mathematician, and millionaire, first proposed this in 1986. It was done through his company NetJets to save costs after reviewing pilot logbooks throughout the years. It was a huge success, and the company expanded across Europe and Russia in the 1990s, eventually becoming the largest business jet operator in Europe by 2006. In later years, the company saw less demand but remained strong in the industry, with an increase around the beginnings of the COVID-19 epidemic.

OWNERSHIP OF A YACHT/BOAT

Small yachts, cabin cruisers, sportfishing yachts, and megayachts are among them. Smaller boats are less expensive these days, but they have fewer options for use. Larger, finer boats are out of reach for a single person. That's where fractional boat ownership comes in, and there are various businesses you can contact to assist you to find exactly what you're looking for and at what percentage you can afford. These firms are useful since you are provided a monthly budget, including yearly increases, so you are fully informed of all costs involved.

You are also offered incentives such as exchanging your time for a new boat and location, which may be a tropical island in another nation depending on the package chosen! Contracts are also easier to get out of because some organizations offer exit points after a set number of years as a customer. Instead of hunting for a new owner, you can use these points to sell the yacht back to the corporation. It's a very affordable way to live a lavish lifestyle on the open sea.

VEHICLES FOR RECREATION

Recreational vehicles (RVs) or mobile homes are immensely popular in the United States, yet they depreciate by up to 30% the instant they are driven off the lot. It is an industry that has required integration into the larger fractional ownership industry.

Today, various companies deal with state-based fractional ownership. They will even find someone to rent out the vehicle for you so that you may profit from your investment during the term of your contract. I say 'contract' because the arrangement is normally for 5 years; after that, the vehicle is sold and the proceeds are divided among the owners. If you choose, you may usually reinvest in a better model at this point.

AUTOMOBILES DE SPORT

It was just a matter of time until you could own a piece of a premium car. Porsche tested this concept in Atlanta in 2018 by giving daily and weekly rentals to see whether anyone was interested. It significantly increased sales, and many other automobile makers have now done the same for their brands and specific models. Companies that deal solely with fractional luxury car ownership have also sprung up, so you have more than just a Porsche to select from and can have a tailor-made plan to suit your budget.

It has become clear that in order for more people to appreciate art, it must be more widely available for purchase. And, considering the enormous cost of owning a work of art, it's no surprise that most individuals can't afford to do so. By owning a share of a piece of art, more art fans may now acquire a beautiful piece and begin learning about the art collection industry without breaking the budget.

This has also allowed experienced collectors to diversify their holdings and galleries to save money on exhibition costs by selling a percentage of high-end pieces.

CHAPTER 3: WHAT ARE NFTS?

NFTs, also known as Nyfties, are blockchain-based digital assets. They have distinguishing characteristics that prevent them from becoming interchangeable. That is, they are difficult to forge, ensuring the legitimacy of the item being acquired.

As technology advanced, so did the simplicity of creating forgeries, duplicating work, and other practices that have lost artists their well-earned salaries for decades. NFTs have aided in resolving the issue that artists all over the world have had in receiving their well-deserved royalties. The ownership of NFTs is recorded on the blockchain, preventing illegitimate copies from being created. This ensures that artists get compensated for their efforts.

As a result, many sorts of NFTs are emerging, such as music, artwork, event tickets, domain names, physical asset ownership, and collectibles. In the present, these are auctioned off in a manner similar to how artwork is sold at a live auction. The only difference is that everything is done online.

NFTs are most commonly found on the Ethereum blockchain, and Ethereum-based tokens are used to validate NFT ownership. Because the item or asset is linked to the token, you can copy the file from someone else's NFT, but it won't be the original, which can be traced. The NFT is owned by whoever holds the token. As a result, each replica or reproduction is confirmed to be a forgery of the original. The token comprises ownership information, an authenticity certificate, and copyright information.

The blockchain is a public registry for digital object ownership that is secure because it cannot be hacked or erased. A ledger entry is established in the same manner as any other blockchain cryptocurrency. This entry contains the file's address, establishing ownership of the NFT. When an NFT is sold, the token code is transferred and recorded as a ledger entry. On the blockchain, this is how ownership is recorded. The NFT owner can add metadata to their new NFT's character. This additional information would specify whether it is art, music, or something else, as well as what format it is in, such as jpeg, video, or something else.

Tokens have no intrinsic value; their worth is determined by the media that is tied to them. Consider an award-winning work of art. The painting's value is determined by the artist's talent and reputation, which is why it is valued for auction. The value is determined by market demand. It is also dependent on scarcity or rarity, because the NFT creator has the option of making duplicates and, if so, how many.

It is critical to remember that the artist retains ownership of the copyright, which they utilize to collect royalties. This is where the information from the previous chapter on fractional ownership comes in handy.

So you own the thing but are unable to reproduce it. It could also be stored on the artist's website, which could be removed. To protect your investment, make sure you understand what happens to the asset if these things happen.

The prices at which numerous digital goods have been sold have made headlines. And the sector has flourished solely because of the rise of bitcoin and the COVID-19 pandemic, which has pushed many products online. People who are unable to attend a concert purchase an exclusive record and view it online.

People were also not spending as much money because they were cooped up inside, didn't have to go to work, and couldn't travel, so they now have extra income to spend. Furthermore, as cryptocurrencies have grown in popularity, one could argue that the stars have aligned for NFT trading.

Its popularity has also aided in the formation of various companies that assist the buying and selling of NFTs, known as NFT Marketplaces, which we shall discuss in detail in Chapter 6. Many investors are paying significant fees to promote NFTs because they believe they will only expand in profitability. With all of this support, it's no surprise that more individuals are interested. Add to it the fact that trading is a simple operation that does not necessitate additional financial support or platforms. For example, if you create digital art, all you have to do is sell it on a marketplace. There's no reason to sell it, spend money marketing it, or risk losing potential purchasers.

I've stated several times that NFTs are not new and have been around for at least a decade. CryptoKitties, digital kittens that were collectibles and immensely popular among cryptocurrency enthusiasts when they were introduced in 2017, are an example of this. Despite the celebrity hoopla, NFTs aren't a passing craze, as seen by the strong trade volume that is continually expanding.

NFTs have been linked to a technology revolution that taps into our desire to own rare and valuable objects without fear of unauthorized reproductions. This is amazing in an age when anything on the internet can and is duplicated. NFTs restore value to items by providing security and traceability.

Despite the news of record-breaking sales, NFT prices have dipped but are remaining consistent even as the enthusiasm fades, giving it a considerably more reliable market in which to invest. It's also unique and novel, which can be a turnoff for many people who are confronted with something that appears to be too wonderful to be true.

This is why there are fears that the NFT market will fall, taking investors with it. However, not everyone is doubtful. NFTs have been compared to the dot-com bubble, when everyone assumed the internet was a passing craze. In truth, all of the hype was driven by overpriced early ventures.

Prices are currently high due to a lot of buzz, but they will fall and stabilize. This is a good thing since it indicates that NFT trading will be around for a long time.

WHAT EXACTLY IS A SPECULATIVE INVESTMENT?

You must conduct research for every form of investment, so it is critical to cover all three types of investments: saving, investing and speculating. You'll be grateful to me later.

SAVE

The first method of investing is to save money. You can, for example, place your money in a savings account to save for a certain item. Although you have the item's value, it is not likely to alter quickly, and you are saving for it. The procedure is gradual, with very little interest growth, but your money is safe because you will not lose any.

If you're saving for a specific purpose and don't want to pay a penalty for early withdrawal from an IRA, you can employ this strategy. These forms of investments, however, primarily include long-term retirement funds.

INVEST

Investing your money simply means that you are accepting a tiny risk when your money begins to increase based on where it is placed. This is a long-term procedure that will take at least three years to complete so that any losses can be offset as earnings improve. Anything shorter will not result in a good trade-off. That's because your money will rise and fall with the market, but not at a frightening rate, and by the end, you'll have weathered the ups and downs and made a fair profit.

This can be accomplished by purchasing stock in a successful company, with the expectation that its success would result in higher returns for you. Most people will only invest with companies that specialize in this, and they will put their money where they believe it will flourish.

SPECULATE

With speculating, you're seeking quick returns in a short amount of time. The risk is substantially larger because you are trying not to lose your money while earning a good return. Day trading is an example of this.

Speculation has been compared to gambling with one's money, yet there is an art to it, and when done correctly, the rewards are spectacular. The idea is to keep an eye on the markets to see what will make the greatest money.

This is not a novel idea; it is utilized for art, collectibles, stocks, and other tangible commodities. The main difference now is that the things are digital rather than tangible, and their authenticity can be verified in a safe setting.

NFTs are classified as speculative investments because their value changes based on what is popular. Because the risks are considerable, it is critical that you comprehend this concept thoroughly as you begin your adventure into NFT trading.

WHAT HAVE BEEN THE MOST EXPENSIVE NFTS SO FAR?

Because the list is constantly changing, I will not list the top ten most expensive NFTs to date, but rather some of the most significant NFTs to date, based not only on their price but also on their rarity and originality.

THE FIRST 5,000 DAYS OF BEEPLE WITH EVERYDAYS

This piece of NFT art was sold at Christie's for $69 million, making it the highest money ever paid for an NFT and the most expensive work of art by a living artist. It consists of 500 pieces of art that were created in May 2007. Vignesh Sundaresan, popularly known as MetaKovan, purchased the artwork and placed it at a digital art museum in the Metaverse, a shared virtual world.

STAY FREE, EDWARD SNOWDEN (EDWARD SNOWDEN 2021)

This artwork displays Edward Snowden's image atop court records demonstrating that the National Security Agency in the United States illegally masses surveyed persons. This was a work of charity art that was sold for more than $5.4 million to support the Freedom of the Press Foundation.

Because of this piece of art, this artist is currently the most expensively selling living Canadian artist. It is also unusual in that it generates fresh NFTs every 28 days, each with its own selling value. This is a significant return on investment for the buyer, who might end up with up to 220 distinct NFTs to sell. Don't you think it's worth the $4.1 million if you can get so much more out of it?

KEVIN MCCOY'S QUANTUM

This is a truly one-of-a-kind NFT, as it was the first to be made as recently as 2014. In May 2014, the artist established the token on Namecoin using technologies he developed with coder Anil Dash. They presented this to an audience at New York's New Museum, but the audience laughed.

However, as the saying goes, "Who's laughing now?" I'd guess the $1.4 million has the two designers smiling all the way to the bank.

WITH THE SWITCH PAK

The owner of this piece of artwork has the option of replacing the artwork with a fresh unknown image. This is part of the artist's representation of how art is evolving online. However, once the new owner decides to activate the switch, it cannot be reversed.

It was sold at Sotheby's for $17 million as part of a collection of seven pieces of digital art, so I can understand why the owner would be afraid to update the item.

WITH GUNKY'S UPRISING, 3LAU

This project is a combination of animated artwork and a music video made to commemorate the third anniversary of the disc jockey and electronic musician's album Ultraviolet. It's no surprise that he has a couple more artworks on sale for $1.3 million. When purchased, these offer unreleased music with the ability for the buyer to name the tracks as well.

DON DIABLO'S JOURNEY TO HEXAGONIA

This full-length, one-hour concert was created by this Dutch DJ, record producer, musician, and songwriter recognized for his electronic music. The owner gets a hard drive holding the only copy of the file based on a Sci-Fi theme. This makes it a highly uncommon collectible, well worth the $1.2 million price tag.

NFT comic books are now being created by Don Diablo.

These NFTs were released on the Ethereum blockchain in 2017 and were inspired by the London punk scene, the cyberpunk movement, and various literature and movies. These are limited to 10,000 characters (6,039 males and 3,840 girls) and are generated by computer code, ensuring that no two characters are identical. Some have even rarer characteristics, making them valuable treasures. Humans, zombies, apes, and alien CryptoPunks are among those with these characteristics, with the latter three being the rarest and most expensive.

This is especially true given the recent surge in NFT sales. They could be accessed for free a few years ago by anyone having an Ethereum wallet. They can now be acquired for as much as $7.58 million each.

WITH THE FIRST-EVER TWEET, JACK DORSEY

Twitter CEO Jack Dorsey has also gotten on the bandwagon, selling his and Twitter's first-ever tweet for $2.9 million. The tweet was sent on March 6, 2006, and it was later sold on the Valuables platform. It was bought by a Malaysian businessman who coveted it and compared it to having Da Vinci's Mona Lisa.

This is exactly how NFTs are perceived: as valuable and uncommon works of art.

The Ethereum money is used in this online video game, which allows players to trade, collect, breed, raise, and battle creatures known as 'axies.' All of the characters are NFTs, and a virtual estate from the game was sold for $1.5 million in February 2021: virtual estate from a video game.

As a result, it was the largest digital land sale ever recorded on the blockchain.

WIFI

NFTs are primarily used to sell exclusive, digital things online, therefore it may be a graphics interchange format (GIF) file or a domain name for which you have the token and location but cannot physically touch. NFTs have the capability of verifying physical goods as proof of ownership. This category includes items such as artwork and real estate.

PROPERTY FOR SALE

Because NFTs include a digital certificate as proof of ownership that cannot be forged or lost, they have grown in popularity in the real estate business and are poised to become the industry standard for such transactions.

First, unlike a traditional deed, NFTs incorporate proof-of-ownership, contractual terms of what can be done to the property, and the foundation for purchasing and selling into a single package.

Second, it eliminates the need for brokers, making properties more accessible online, not to mention transaction security and traceability.

It's not just a theory; in 2021, the world's first real estate NFT was successfully sold. It's an apartment in Kyiv, Ukraine, that made history in 2017 when it became the first property to be sold and purchased using blockchain technology. The now-former owner opted to sell it as an NFT in order to demonstrate the value of blockchain technology in the real estate business.

The NFT featured three items: access to the ownership documentation, a photograph of the apartment, and another NFT in the form of digital art by a well-known artist. The tangible painting of this art was painted on the apartment wall and can be seen in the apartment image.

Because the property is in Ukraine, but the new owner is in America, this was an international transaction. As a result, the property had to be kept and recorded in Ukraine first as a United States limited liability company (LLC). Because the NFT included rights to the LLC, the transition to the new owner went smoothly.

This transaction has now cleared the way for future real estate deals.

There are entire worlds that have been developed for you to explore, create, and purchase stuff in. It's analogous to playing a real-time online video game in which you are the main character. They have grown in popularity since the physical distance is no longer an impediment to communication and interaction.

Trading digital assets have exploded in these virtual worlds, accounting for 20% of the NFT market to date. In these universes, real estate acquisitions in the form of NFTs ranging from $1.5 million to $2.8 million are common.

Many of you may be unfamiliar with the term "virtual reality," let alone "virtual worlds," so I'll go through it in more detail.

VIRTUAL REALITY

The concept of virtual reality was first seen in science fiction books envisioning a world full of robots and flying cars. But it is now very much a part of the world, and technology is continually advancing.

Virtual reality is a simulation, a copy of a real-world event, such as mountain climbing, or something altogether different, such as a sword fight on a ship on the open seas. It's not simply for pleasure, but also for education, such as military or medical training, such as flight simulators for pilots or virtual business meetings, which have skyrocketed since the Covid-19 pandemic.

We've all been on a ZOOM call where someone has a virtual background, such as a beach in Bali when you know they reside in a Brooklyn flat. The technology currently incorporates augmented reality (interaction with objects in real-world situations) and mixed reality (interaction with both real and virtual worlds), also known as 'extended reality.'

Movies like Tron, Johnny Mnemonic, and The Matrix are excellent examples, albeit a touch old.

EQUIPMENT

The first mounted virtual reality system was available in the 1960s, and it was followed by a couple of commercial models until the 1980s when it began to decline. It has accelerated since 2010, with the creation of Oculus Rift, which took years to develop until its release in 2016.

The device resembles a thick set of goggles that cover your eyes and must be connected to a computer or a cell phone. To navigate, the user must also wear headphones and use hand controllers and other peripherals. Consider moving around in a dream yet having control over your activities.

The Oculus Rift is a range of virtual reality headsets that have been decommissioned to make room for their successors, the most recent model being the Oculus Quest 2, which has been in operation since October 13, 2020. This headset allows the user to enter a virtual world, either fantasy-based or reality-based, such as mountain-climbing games. It is intended to completely immerse the user, making them believe they are in that environment, experiencing everything.

There's even the Samsung Gear VR, which wraps around Samsung devices to provide a less expensive virtual reality experience. As numerous corporations have begun to create their own products, the choice is vast and appeals to a wide range of tastes and budgets.

THE METAVERSE

The term *"metaverse" refers to shared virtual environments.* The term is used to define what the internet aspires to be. It was first used in Neal Stephenson's 1992 novel Snow Crash, which imagined a virtual environment with which users may interact. With the growing popularity of NFTs and the creation of so many virtual worlds for people to interact with, technology is attempting to integrate the two so that they may all be shared.

The current owner of the most costly NFT to date, the artwork Everydays: The First 5,000 Days, intends to display it across four virtual worlds so that people can view and enjoy it in more than one location. And things of all types are bought and sold within these virtual worlds. Taco Bell, for example, is creating and has been developing items for this market. It's completely another type of retail.

DECENTRALAND

To date, Decentraland is the most popular virtual world. It is a community-based platform that allows users to own plots of land, artwork, and NFTs in the form of various items, including collectibles. Users are also given the opportunity to participate in its governance.

It began in 2016 with a 2D model and has since grown to become one of the largest 3D worlds available. It has its own coinage, called 'mana,' which is stored on Ethereum's blockchain alongside the game's assets.

Decentraland differs from other online games in that the rules of the game are controlled by the players. When you join, you also become a member of the Decentralized Autonomous Organization (DAO), which allows you to vote on numerous issues that affect the game's structure or policies. There is a marketplace for selling and buying NFTs ranging from in-game trinkets to clothing and land. You may show off your NFT art, exchange stuff, and even monetize your territory; the possibilities are limitless.

As previously stated in relation to the Metaverse, products of all types are bought and sold within these virtual worlds. Adidas had a fashion show in Decentraland, and the designs were sold as NFTs. Fashion firms and sports brands are increasingly staging on displays and advertising their virtual designs.

LOANS

An NFT can now be used as collateral for a loan. Numerous marketplaces, such as Hoard Exchange, are running beta websites for this function, and several financial institutions, such as Lamna Financial in South Africa, have begun to issue NFT loans. The explanation is based on the rise of bitcoin and digital technology, which has caused clients to change their behavior. Financial organizations do not want to fall behind in order to stay competitive.

NFT VARIETIES

There are many different types of NFTs, and more are being developed all the time because the possibilities are essentially limitless. Anything you can conceive of maybe or is already an NFT.

ART

Digital designs, films, GIFs, pictures, memes, social media content, and pixels are the most popular types of NFTs. In the coming chapters, we will go over this sort of NFT in greater detail, as well as how to trade it successfully.

ARTICLES

Several New York Times and Quartz articles have been marketed as NFTs. One came from journalist Kevin Roose, who wrote an essay about selling the story and then auctioned it off as a non-fiction piece for $560,000.

Although not a news piece, it is worth noting that The Associated Press was the first news company to sell their artwork for $180,000. The Associated Press refers to it as the 2020 presidential election on blockchain— Outer Space Perspective

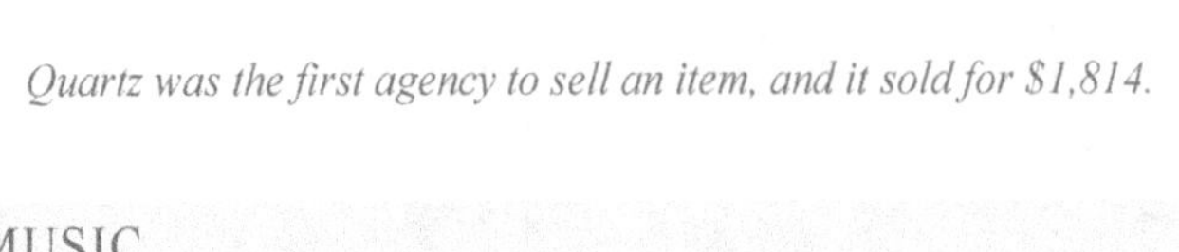

Quartz was the first agency to sell an item, and it sold for $1,814.

MUSIC

Kings of Leon were the first to release their record as an NFT in March 2021, earning the band a cool $2 million. They were not, however, the only ones; many musicians have begun digitizing their work as a result of this new money stream.

Linkin Park's Mike Shinoda, Grimes, DJ Steve Aoki, and many others have since used various marketplace channels to bring their art to fans, with great success.

PLAYING CARDS

These are digital representations of physical collectors cards, such as baseball cards or tabletop game cards.

The NBA was the first in the sports world to launch NFTs, which featured highlights from fans' favorite basketball teams. These were packaged in the style of digital trading cards and were a major success, earning over $390 million since their October 2020 launch. NFTs can now be found in boxing and Formula One, among other sports that are taking an interest.

VIDEO GAMES/METAVERSE

We discussed the metaverse and virtual reality environments, such as Decentraland, where NFTs abound in all kinds. The most frequent, though, are those that enhance the gaming experience. Avatars, which are video game characters that the user creates to look like whatever they like, allow the player to change their appearance as much as they want. You can also get skins, which change the appearance of the avatar but have no effect on gameplay, similar to having a haircut.

Finally, there are collectibles, which are frequently concealed items that provide users with a bonus of some kind, such as a sword or rifle. These are not essential to complete game stages, but they provide excellent bonuses and are well worth the hunt.

Designer fashion businesses have begun to offer digital luxury fashion goods based on the same principle as avatar clothes. For those who can afford it, your virtual self can now buy a pair of Gucci sneakers. It's not a ridiculous idea, anyway, considering high fashion is primarily about individuality and exclusivity. That ideal can now be celebrated in a virtual environment as well.

On June 29, 2021, the world's first virtual mall opened, allowing users to browse virtual businesses and make purchases. It's known as Metajuka, and it's growing as more fashion houses and designers join the NFT fashion craze.

DOMAIN NAMES

Previously, an organization was in charge of buying and selling domain names, but now the new owner only requires the private keys in the NFT.

Domain names connected to cryptocurrencies are extremely popular and command high prices because everyone wants to possess one. Of course, NFT domain names are popular right now because you can't enter the market until you have the right moniker. Unstoppable Domain sold the most expensive domain name, "win.crypto," for $100,000.

The technology is also evolving because domain names may be used to connect crypto wallets, making it easier to send and receive cryptocurrency.

FILM

Deadpool 2 digital posters, as well as the Oscar-nominated Claude Lanzmann: Spectres of the Shoah, were released in March 2021. The latter was the first motion picture, documentary, and Oscar-nominated film to be auctioned off as an NFT.

But that's not all the film industry has to offer. Anthony Hopkins' latest film Zero Contact will be released as an NFT on the Vuele platform for the first time. This is something to look forward to, as there will be multiple copies, each with its own set of bonuses and priced differently. According to the director, Rick Dugdal, this suggests the film will be distributed in a 'limited edition.'

MEMES

If you haven't heard of memes, they are ideas, habits, or styles that take the shape of hilarious visuals and are spread through social media. Several popular memes, like Doge (a picture of a Shiba Inu dog), Nyan Cat, and Disaster Girl, have been minted as NFTs and sold for as much as $4 million each.

The reason for this is simple: wealthy collectors want to gather early internet history, not just how it appeared when it went popular, but also how it started and from where it came. That's why the iconic Harambe meme was found, and the photographer, Jeff McCurry, is going to make history by selling the original shot as an NFT.

PORNOGRAPHY

Popular porn performers have also begun to transform their work into NFTs as part of their efforts to provide new content to their customers. Other NFT marketplaces have been less than enthusiastic about this and the sector as a whole, although these NFTs do exist. As a result, marketplaces for this form of NFT have sprung up, with their own auctions, establishing a new niche in the adult industry.

ACADEMIA

Because research money isn't always easy to come by, Yale's Department of Statistics and Data Science (S&DS) has devised a workaround: it is auditioning its first NFT. It was intended to memorialize Francis Anscombe's renowned research piece, Anscombe's Quartet, which was published in 1973. He was the first chair of Yale's Department of Statistics. It is most typically used to teach researchers the importance of charting data before studying it. It's not the only piece of academic literature being issued as an NFT. The University of California Berkeley has issued patent disclosures for CRISPR-Cas9 gene editing and cancer immunotherapy as NFTs, which will be sold for $55,000 on June 8, 2021.

This paves the path for more research articles to attract much-needed financing.

TOKENS FOR SOCIAL GOOD

These are tokens based on a brand, community, or influencer that are issued by individuals and communities. Some have used it to pay for their time, such as an hour of consulting. Others have utilized it to award followers for their participation. It is a means for celebrities and influencers to monetize their time spent with their fans or followers, and it is a very profitable way to earn money through notoriety.

Many NFTs are built on the Ethereum blockchain and are paid for with its ETH currency. But it doesn't imply they have to keep shifting about in order to be sold. The NFT is stored in a virtual wallet that travels with the person to various platforms, granting them access to this wallet. A program such as MetaMask is required so that each platform can access this wallet and allow for smooth purchasing and selling.

Various marketplaces, such as OpenSea and Mintbase, allow you to create NFTs without paying any costs. Each of these comes with its own set of step-by-step instructions for using the site.

Most marketplace platforms charge you a fee known as a "gas fee" to cover the expense of creating or minting the NFT. These fees fluctuate regularly and can be costly. However, after these fees have been paid and the NFT has been uploaded to a website, it has been created and is ready to be sold.

HISTORY AND KEY IDEAS

Most books and articles discuss the rise of NFTs and their origins, beginning with CryptoKitties. I tried something similar a few chapters back. However, the concept was formed much earlier, therefore I will now take you on that journey. Let's take a look at the history of NFTs and the key concepts that have shaped them into what they are now.

COLORED BITCOIN COINS

In 2012, colored Bitcoin coins were used to exchange meme artwork. They were also referred to as 'satoshis' the smallest unit of Bitcoin and equal to one-hundredth of a Bitcoin. They were also called after the creator of Bitcoin, Satoshi Nakamoto.

These colorful coins were only used in extremely tiny circles and were hence uncommon. They were short-lived because they could only reflect a value if everyone agreed on it. When an agreement could not be reached, this produced serious transaction complications.

QUANTUM

Kevin McCoy and Anil Dash established a framework for the existence of digital art. They attempted this in 2014 and submitted their concept, but it was rejected. Because of this, they never patented their blockchain notion and hence do not control the technology today.

They are not, however, forgotten, and Anil Dash is still active in bitcoin and startup circles. He is not yet ready to sell the original presentation video as an NFT. But Kevin McCoy was eager to sell Quantum, which is recognized for what it is and how it aided in the development of technology and the eventual establishment of NFT.

COUNTERPARTY

CounterParty is a peer-to-peer financial platform that was established on the blockchain in 2014. It is concerned with the exchange of memes and card games. The company was founded because the founders believed in blockchain technology but were unsure how significant a role it would play.

Between 2015 and 2016, when memes began to be marketed, beginning with Pepe Frog, CounterParty noticed an increase in users. Rare photos of this meme became the thing to collect, and individuals were willing to spend a lot of money to obtain a rare Pepe Frog. This success persuaded the founders of Force of Will to work together on the platform in 2016.

At the time, Force of Will was a popular trading card game, and they needed a venue to sell their cards. This resulted in an additional spike of sales, demonstrating the benefit of being able to acquire and sell such collections online and with simplicity.

ETHEREUM

Ethereum was launched in 2017 as much more than a cryptocurrency. The startup made its own headlines based on what it could accomplish, but things really took off with the release of CryptoKitties. This was an NFT game on the Ethereum platform that allowed users to use blockchain technology to breed unusual digital cats.

The game's popularity acted as a spur for NFTs to take center stage. It was so popular that it drew a lot of media attention and, in a way, got more people interested in online collecting.

This gave rise to **CryptoPunks**, and the list of items you can buy and trade on various marketplace platforms is now unlimited, depending on what you wish to collect.

THE PROBLEM OF CARBON EMISSIONS

I can't discuss how NFTs are made without mentioning the issue of carbon emissions. It would be irresponsible of me not to mention it because you will encounter it when you begin trading in NFTs or in any debate regarding bitcoin.

Because they are formed using blockchain transactions that adhere to the proof-of-work protocol, NFTs necessitate a significant amount of computational power. Simply said, one side proves to the other that a particular quantity of labor was completed. It is demonstrated by completing a mathematical problem or transaction. It appears to be complicated, and it is. All of this is done, however, with computers that run these equations in the background with the assistance of specific software. The people running these computers, known as miners, are compensated in cryptocurrency for solving these equations, so there is an incentive to keep a large number of processors working at all times.

Transactions are completed at a quick pace, giving rise to server farms built specifically for this purpose around the world. Because server farms are generally located in nations with low electricity costs, they rely heavily on fossil fuels to generate electricity. As a result, there is a significant carbon footprint, which is prompting a lot of opposition to NFT usage. It's the fundamental reason why, despite their popularity, many people are hesitant to manufacture and sell NFTs.

Ethereum mining is believed to consume as much electricity as the country of Ireland, while a 2018 study discovered that cryptocurrency mining consumes more energy than gold or copper extraction (de la Garza, 2021). Even with this research, it is difficult to assess an NFT's carbon footprint because there are so many variables to consider. Blockchain miners, who run these computers, are spread across the globe, making it difficult to determine how much energy is being consumed at any particular time. As a result, estimating the carbon footprint of each NFT is now difficult. That doesn't imply there isn't an impact or that there isn't cause for concern.

It is a major topic of discussion, particularly in relation to climate change. The general opinion is that the energy used must be green. Cryptocurrency firms have reached an agreement, and the majority of them are working hard to make adjustments. There are also green marketplace systems that sell themselves in this manner.

Companies such as the Ethereum platform are also looking into ways to modify the way the currency is mined and drastically reduce its carbon impact.

ECO-FRIENDLY IDEAS

All mining could be done with renewable resources, but for a variety of reasons, it isn't. The main reason is that many countries use fossil fuels, and the electricity produced is quite inexpensive. That is why many server farms are located in those countries: the incentive to mine is extremely lucrative. Because of the infrastructure expenses to construct these renewable energy sources, it would be difficult to shut down large mining operations and force them to use solar or wind power.

As a result, newer blockchain technologies have begun to integrate alternate validation procedures, such as proof-of-stake, which needs far less energy for each transaction. Ethereum is attempting to replace mining with staking, which uses far less energy. When this principle is applied to all of its transactions, it will save up to 99.98 percent of its energy (Ethereum, n.d.)

Fortunately, this isn't simply a pipe dream because the technology is already being constructed and used on a smaller scale on other platforms. It simply needs to be able to handle larger transactions and work in the backend.

PROOF-OF-STAKE

I described how the proof-of-work system works and why cryptocurrency entrepreneurs are aiming to replace it with proof-of-stake. But what exactly is proof-of-stake?

Transactions must still be authenticated before new blocks can be produced; this does not change. However, because the energy usage is low, the validation of these transactions does not necessitate a large mining capacity. The hardware required to perform these transactions is also modest, resulting in low energy usage. Validators earn transaction fees rather than block rewards, thus the benefits are distinct, scalable, and do not encourage big server farm mining.

Validators must stake a particular amount of cryptocurrency in order to become validators. For Ethereum, that amount is 32 ETH, after which random validators are selected to either produce a new block or examine and confirm existing blocks. There are other consequences. These penalties reward good validator behavior but not high computation power. Validators lose a piece of their investment if they do not complete the work or do it incorrectly.

The blockchain is not vulnerable to a 51 percent attack, which is a significant security benefit of utilizing this method of validation. This is only possible if a miner or mining pool controls 51% of the network's transaction-solving power and then begins producing fraudulent blocks that benefit itself while invalidating those that do not. With proof-of-stake, no one, not even a hacker, would be able to hold 51 percent of the bitcoin network, and even if they did, attacking would be pointless because it would also target their share.

TRANSACTIONS IN THE OFF-CHAIN

Off-chain transactions are those that occur outside of the blockchain. They can function by transferring private keys to an existing wallet or by utilizing a third party. This is what PayPal undertakes to ensure that its transactions are honored. Off-chain transactions can be completed instantly, with no transaction fees and improved security. However, these must be put to the blockchain at some point in order to be recorded on the ledger. So there is a cost, but it is not prohibitively expensive.

At the present, the main price is that it trades dependability, transparency, and decentralization, all of which the blockchain and cryptocurrencies were designed to achieve.

CHAPTER 6: CREATING NFTS

Now that you understand how it all began and how it works, you can begin making your own NFTs. First, I'll walk you through the processes required to get started as a digital artist. This chapter will go over how to sell your artwork later on.

HOW TO MAKE A LIVING AS A CRYPTO ARTIST

It's not impossible just because you didn't start out as a digital artist. It can be more difficult when you are not widely known, but I have some hints and tips that may help.

I AM NOT A DIGITAL ARTIST.

If you are a physical artwork artist, you must first master the tools and have the software before you can consider generating NFTs. There are several options available, depending on the devices you intend to use and whether you intend to print the artwork as well.

Some people have taken their physical work and run it through software to add animations before turning it into NFTs, so if you don't want to spend the time learning about tools and establishing a digital portfolio from scratch, that is a possibility for you.

You can also avoid all of that by selling your actual artwork as an NFT.

You must determine whether the physical copy, the digital copy, or both are unique assets. Both can be marketed as one-of-a-kind items, but how you list them is critical. The reason for this is that NFTs are one-of-a-kind artifacts that command high prices. They are collectible due to the scarcity value they bring.

As a result, one alternative is to destroy the actual artwork after scanning it, which is a regular process that adds value to the NFT. You may alternatively simply designate the original to be a tool used in the creation process and not for sale. There are numerous possibilities available; it all depends on what you want to do.

A digital SLR camera is required because it will provide the finest quality, therefore investing in this piece of equipment is critical. Instead of purchasing your own equipment, you may hire a photographer. Make sure there is plenty of natural light or adequate lighting. You could also scan your artwork and digitize it using specialized software and a specialized scanner. This is only possible if your artwork is small enough to scan and is scanned at a high dot-per-inch resolution.

ARE YOU ALREADY A DIGITAL ARTIST?

These instructions are for someone who is already familiar with digital artwork tools and simply needs to adapt them to NFTs.

If you are already a digital artist, you should establish a name or brand for yourself. This is critical later on for building NFTs. If not, now is a good moment to come up with a catchy name or brand that you don't think will alter in the future. You don't want to use your own name; instead, choose a pseudonym that you like and would be delighted to keep for years.

The next stage is to decide what you want to make. You should have an idea based on previous work, even if you haven't sold anything professionally. A good way to figure this out is to organize your physical artwork and label it by genre, style, message, or whatever suits you best. Then, choose your best piece or design a new piece based on your strong features.

After you've decided on your piece, you'll need to pick on the format, such as GIFs, videos, motion graphics, and so on. Will it simply be a piece of digital art, or will it be animated or in motion?

You can now begin making your masterpiece and uploading it to a marketplace. Later in the chapter, I'll walk you through these steps. After you've launched an NFT on your preferred marketplace platform, there are two critical actions you should take as a new artist: joining a community and advertising your work.

PARTICIPATING IN A COMMUNITY

This is critical for emerging artists since you will receive essential knowledge on topics such as new technologies, market changes, and any trends that may be relevant to how you want your art to evolve.

Join organizations that encourage new artists, such as Crypto Arts, Arts Rights, and Art Concierge. You're going to need some help to get your art out there and sell it.

HOW TO MARKET YOUR DIGITAL ART

In addition to seeking community aid, use your social media profiles and friends and family to spread the message. You won't make millions right away, but the goal is to build a fan base and then see how well your art sells.

STORIES OF SUCCESS

After years of hardship, many artists of various ages and nations have discovered this to be a very profitable venture. Their stories are both motivating and one-of-a-kind.

BLACKSNEAKERS

JAZMINE BOYKINS

, A student at North Carolina A&T State University, used to share her artwork for free on the internet. Her only source of income was from selling swag at her institution. Her artwork is now selling for thousands of dollars as NFTs, and she has earned $60,000 in six months. Her online alias is Blacksneakers, and her earnings have given her the confidence to continue.

Andrew Benson, who lives in Los Angeles, retained his day job because, despite the fact that his art was displayed in museums and he collaborated with musicians, he wasn't making enough to quit his day job at a software business.

Benson's intentions to exhibit went through when the epidemic struck, making him question whether it was all worth it. His acquaintance, who works at Foundation, requested him to submit a piece in January 2021. It was sold for $1,250 within 10 days. That prompted Benson to submit ten more works, all of which sold in the same price range. It appears like his future is brightening.

This Canadian artist toiled for years before becoming an artist at a late age. Despite this, Trevor Jones continued to strive to break into the art industry, and it wasn't until he was in his 40s that he was able to begin creating artwork based on technology. This was all part of finding his specialty, which he achieved.

Jones began using augmented reality (AR) to bring what appeared to be conventional artwork to life. As more of his paintings began to sell, he began to gain a following. By 2019, he was painting portraits of notable people, particularly those associated with the cryptocurrency world.

KnownOrigin approached Jones about creating NFTs on their platform. And the rest, as they say, is history. It's quite an accomplishment to go from being a struggling artist for years to becoming well-known in a matter of years.

GXNGYXNG

Since he was a child, this artist had been doing hand-drawn work and getting in trouble at school. His name is Gong Yang, and he has always wanted to be an animator, so he studied 3D and 2D animation and began working at an animation studio to realize his ambition. He liked it because it allowed him to be creative, but he didn't like it because he wasn't working for himself.

GxngYxng has now amassed a collection of 1,000 works and has resigned from his day job.

CHOOSING A PLATFORM FOR A MARKETPLACE

It is critical to select a platform that works best for you. Because there are so many options, I'll list some of the most user-friendly, but ultimately, you should explore what's available and select the one with which you're most comfortable.

If you are an established digital artist with a sizable fanbase, you should choose Nifty Gateway, Knoworigin, SuperRare, Rarible, or Foundation.

The first three are invite-only, but you may be invited to join if you have a portfolio of your work and enough individuals supporting it. There is an application process, and if these marketplaces want your work, you can be up-voted.

Coinbase and eToro are wonderful venues for beginner traders if all you want to do is trade.

FEES FOR GAS

It is not always free to build an NFT, as many marketplace platforms charge a gas fee to cover the cost of constructing the NFT on Ethereum's blockchain. Nifty Gateway charges 5% plus an extra $0.30 for each subsequent secondary sale. The most expensive is foundation, which can cost up to 15% if you need it done rapidly against a busy network.

Fees fluctuate often, so it's always a good idea to maintain some cryptocurrency in your virtual wallet to cover these extra expenditures. Set aside enough money for these costs to cover the production of one NFT unless you intend to create a large number of them at once. You should be fine with $100 or so, but because fees change frequently, have at least double that amount on hand.

POPULAR SHOPPING MALLS

There are several marketplace systems, with new ones appearing all the time. Many platforms include secondary marketplaces, and each platform might work differently based on what it's for and what the marketplace hopes to accomplish.

INVENTIVE GATEWAY

This marketplace is controlled by Gemini, a well-known bitcoin exchange. It collaborates with well-known musicians such as DJ Steve Aoki, Grimes, and 3LAU. It also includes a secondary market where collectors may resell their artwork. Artists can choose the percentages they want from these secondary sales in this marketplace.

To utilize the website as you would any other online purchase, you can either use ETH tokens or attach a credit card. This makes it easier to use because you don't need any bitcoin to sign up and purchase an item.

Limited-edition collections are made that are only accessible for a limited time, referred to as a drop.

You can submit a blind bid and wait to see if you won in an online silent auction.

Draw: similar to a raffle or lottery, you gain an advantage based on the number of entries you submit. It was also designed to be a hindrance to bots obtaining top NFTs.

Open edition: during 5 to 15 minutes, an infinite number of NFTs are accessible on a piece, making it available to everybody.

Global offer: You can submit an offer that the owners will review and decide whether or not to accept; this is available to anyone in the world.

To sell an NFT, use **MetaMask** to upload it to your Nifty Gateway omnibus wallet. This is the only way you'll be able to do it. If you want to become a creator to sell, you must first apply via an eight-part questionnaire on the website, followed by an interview.

ATOMICMARKET

This is a one-of-a-kind marketplace platform since it is a shared liquidity NFT market smart contract. The term "shared liquidity" refers to the fact that anything listed on one marketplace platform appears on other marketplace platforms as well. A smart contract is a blockchain application that conducts actions based on certain conditions being met. When registering a vehicle, for example, all of the details are entered by the user, and the registration is completed.

AtomicMarket is used by a variety of websites to provide users with a one-of-a-kind and enjoyable experience. AtomicAssets is the term given to NFTs, and it is one of the few platforms that verifies well-known collections. This ensures that you are purchasing the authentic article. It is highly picky about its collections and will ban any malicious collections it discovers.

OPENSEA

Because this is a peer-to-peer platform, individuals engage directly with one another without the intervention of a third party. It bills itself as a supplier of rare digital things and collectibles, and it only charges a 2.5 percent gas fee after the transaction. If you establish an account to browse the NFT collections, you can sort them by sales volume to find new artists.

It runs *on Ethereum,* but users can sell in any money they like, and they can even add their own currency by contacting the firm and requesting that it be featured. This platform also enables users to buy, sell, and explore virtual worlds such as Decentraland, Axis, and others.

SUPERRARE

This marketplace functions more like a social network, but it also serves as a marketplace for the buying and trading of rare and unique NFTs. Because Ethereum is the cryptocurrency used on it, you must first purchase the currency ETH before you can make purchases on the platform. SuperRare levies a purchasing fee of *3%*, which customers must pay.

It is unique in that each piece of art shown is a one-of-a-kind edition, increasing its uniqueness value. It is continually evolving to become more sociable, and the tailored notifications on its home page have been modified. These include an activity feed to bring users up to date on everything they should be aware of.

It's an excellent forum for artists that are just starting out and have new and imaginative artwork.

BAKERYSWAP

BakerySwap is more than simply an NFT marketplace platform; it's a multipurpose crypto hub that provides a wide range of decentralized financial services as well as a crypto launchpad.

A crypto launchpad is a location where new projects can raise funding. It also allows investors to acquire early access to these projects as well as tokens at a discounted price before they are released. It's an excellent strategy to entice investors. Crypto launchpads also examine new initiatives, ensuring that investors are not jeopardized.

BakerySwap has its own NFT tokens called BAKE, which are used when the site hosts digital art, meme competitions, and NFTs in games. It is believed to be one of the most user-friendly NFT platforms for minting and selling artwork.

RARIBLE

Rarible, like OpenSea, is an open marketplace for artists and producers to issue and sell NFTs. In reality, Rarible's platform allows you to view and manage your OpenSea collectibles.

It has its own token, known as the RARI. These are granted to users who want to have a say on its platforms, such as fees and community regulations. Users that want to contribute to the platform's development buy these tokens in order to be more actively involved and not only utilize them as a marketplace. You can opt to keep your NFT until you're ready to sell it, gift it to someone, or even have it utterly destroyed utilizing the platform.

This is a private community that does not allow anyone to utilize its platform. To obtain entry, artists must either acquire an invitation from other creators on the platform or receive up-votes. This simply means that creators on the site can nominate someone and the community votes on whether or not they can post their work.

When an artist is granted the go-ahead to join, they must purchase gas in order to mint their NFTs. This implies they must pay the cost of manufacturing the NFT in cryptocurrency, and prices fluctuate. All of these requirements ensure that this platform is very exclusive and has very good work on its platform, ensuring that buyers pay higher prices.

Another fascinating feature of Foundation is that it isn't simply about creating, purchasing, and selling NFTs. It is also significantly involved in allowing artists to explore and build things similar to hackathons, which bring together creative people to create something new by playing with technology.

CARGO

This marketplace is somewhat obscure in the media, yet it is a good starting point for newcomers. It also accepts the ETH cryptocurrency, however, anyone may open an account and start minting NFTs. The first distinguishing aspect is that there are no auctions; artists price their work and anyone who likes it can purchase it.

The second distinguishing feature is the ability to split royalties, allowing musicians to collaborate and share earnings because up to 15 unique wallet addresses can be linked to a single NFT. There are no gas fees because it uses a function known as 'magic minting,' and it is a simple platform to use.

Myth GPK.Market, GoPepe.Market, KOGS.Market, and Shatner.Market are all part of the Market umbrella marketplace. It's no surprise they refer to themselves as a "series of simple internet markets." This simply means that these other markets run on this platform, and you can choose which one you wish to trade on.

This NFT marketplace platform focuses solely on trading cards, and the only coin supported is WAX. This is an abbreviation for The Worldwide Asset eXchange, which is both a form of blockchain technology and a cryptocurrency. WAX coins may be purchased on the majority of cryptocurrency exchanges.

MINTABLE

Mintable has everything that can be an NFT, including art, music, game goods, collectibles, and more. It, too, is built on the Ethereum blockchain, but it allows for gasless minting. Users use MINT tokens to participate in the platform's DAO. This allows users to vote on any platform modifications and can be gained through the platform's buying and selling of NFTs or purchased.

There are three sorts of auctions to choose from: time, buy it now, and classic auction. Another distinguishing feature is its interface with OpenSea, which allows you to manage your collections in OpenSea and vice versa, which is especially useful for trade.

MAKING AN NFT

The processes for creating an NFT will vary based on the platform you use. In the following example, we will utilize the Mintable marketplace platform because it is simple to use and popular among newcomers.

MAKE A METAMASK WALLET.

This is a web3 cryptocurrency wallet, which means it has a chrome extension that allows you to engage with your preferred NFT marketplace platform.

MetaMask is the most widely used, and it is where all of your digital cash will be stored. Formatic, Coinbase, Wallet, Torus, and Portis are some other wallets to consider.

Before you can create an account on most platforms, you must first purchase ETH and have some in your wallet. This is for gas fees if the platform charges them.

MAKE AN ACCOUNT

Once you've decided on a marketplace platform, either from the list I've provided or from your own research, you'll need to sign up for an account, just as you would with any other website. In this phase, you will have the opportunity to provide access to your MetaMask wallet.

CREATING THE NFT

The processes I've outlined are subject to change and may differ from those of other marketplace platforms.

- *'Mint an Item'* is located at the top of the Mintable website. Choose that.

- *Choose "Create a new item."*

- Depending on whether you want to pay expensive fees, choose either traditional or gasless. For this example, we'll use the usual option.

- *Select the sort of item you want to transform into an NFT. Art, collectibles, gaming objects, music, domains, templates, and videos are all choices. We'll go with the collectible route.*

- *In the Mintable Store,* you'll see a box next to the words Mint that you can check if you want. This simply means that if you click in the box, whatever you convert into an NFT will be added to Mintable's collection, and most platforms have this option. Because you are not paying to host your digital item anyplace, it is the most cost-effective alternative. The only time you would not choose this option is if you are quite well-known and want to maintain your work under your label or brand. When the option is selected, the token address for the item, which is your smart contract for the item, is provided. At this point, the token ID is also provided.

- Unless you have a large number of goods to mint, select *"Only mint my token."*

- *Make up a Token Name, a listing title, and a listing subtitle.*

- You now have the option to upload a private/unlockable item. This is where you can include objects in your NFT that only the owner has access to. This might be a terrific way to make your NFT stand out.

- You can now submit the image that you want to mint into an NFT.

- The next step is to include *"additional metadata,"* such as the data's name and value. However, it is not required to finish the minting, so you can skip this step if you like.

- When you click *"List this item,"* a pop-up window opens informing you that you are about to conduct a blockchain transaction.

- You can either cancel to continue entering information or click "proceed."

- Your MetaMask wallet will then open automatically. It will display the overall gas charges for this NFT creation.

- If you have enough ETH, click "confirm"; otherwise, you must first add some Ether to your wallet.

- When you click *"confirm,"* a pop-up page opens to indicate that you have created an NFT.

- You may view the item from this screen by clicking on it, or you can go to your profile and view it from there.

PUTTING THE NFT ON THE MARKET

- You can sell or transfer the NFT once it has been minted and appears on your profile. If you want it to be for sale, take the following steps:

- You must assign it a category, a listing title, a subtitle, and a description.

- *"Transfer copyright when purchased"* is an important checkbox. That means the owner can utilize the object for commercial purposes without fear of consequences. If you have a cause not to enable copyright movement, this is the place to specify it.

- Then you have the option of allowing the buyer to resell. You don't want to uncheck this option because you want to allow the deal to take place.

- You must also select a fixed price in US dollars that will display the ETH amount beneath it.

- Then, after clicking *"List this item,"* your MetaMask wallet will reopen. It will have its own pop-up screen asking you to sign or cancel the transaction.

- Select *"sign"* and continue.

- You are presented with another pop-up page to confirm the transaction.

- Your NFT is now ready to be sold on Mintable.

THE NFT'S POST-SALE EXPERIENCE

When you sell your artwork and don't transfer the copyright, this is what happens:

You own the copyright as the artist, and the buyer receives a certificate of ownership. This data will alter as the piece is bought and traded, allowing the blockchain to monitor each owner.

If you, as the artist, choose any secondary sale fees, these will be applied here, thus with each resells, you will receive a royalty payment.

CHAPTER 7: NFT TRADING

There are numerous NFT Marketplace sites where you can purchase and sell NFTs by bidding, and some even allow you to acquire free NFTs. Marketplaces similar to bitcoin exchanges are advantageous to acquire from due to the high resale value you may find here.

High-demand NFTs may have a high resale value right after they are published, but you can't tell until you use this type of marketplace. The rationale for this is that you will be able to compare previous transactions to evaluate resale demand.

In this chapter, I'll walk you through the several marketplaces that sell the greatest NFTs per category, followed by a description of a couple to consider for resale. This allows you to go through the many types and begin trading.

Before you can begin trading, you must first answer a few questions.

- TO PURCHASE NFTS, WHICH NFT MARKETPLACE PLATFORM SHOULD I USE?

Because there are a variety of NFTs to invest in, I've mentioned where you can acquire NFTs for various goods that are suitable for trading, as well as particular ones for art trading options.

]

WHAT COIN IS REQUIRED TO PURCHASE THESE NFTS?

Most are based on Ethereum, hence the currency is ETH. Some accept different currencies, and a few allow you to pay with your credit card. You should check each platform's FAQ page because it changes as the platforms evolve.

ARE THE NFTS ONLY ACCESSIBLE IN A LIMITED QUANTITY?

Drops are limited sales in which artists offer a collection or a piece of artwork on that marketplace for a certain price for a set period of time.

These types of sales can be helpful for trading because only uncommon items are sold this way, thus you want to buy when these drops occur. However, don't merely buy something at a high price and expect a huge return. See what goods are popular and stick to them, but don't overspend.

BASKETBALL

NBA Top Shot was developed for licensed collectibles and is concerned with digital, collectible basketball cards that are significantly more dynamic than traditional trading cards. They include in-game highlights for each of the featured players. The most popular card was one for LeBron James, which featured a video of him dunking on the Houston Rockets. It was known as the LeBron James Dunk card, and it sold for $200,000 at auction (Conti, 2021).

This industry is quite popular right now, and if you're a basketball enthusiast, you won't have to look far to find out that digital cards are on the rise. Even if you are not a basketball enthusiast, you will be able to determine which teams are the greatest and which players are the best in order to determine which cards will bring you the most profit.

VIDEO GAMES

Online video games have grown in popularity over the years, to the point where one can earn a job solely by playing video games. Professional gaming has actually advanced to a new level with Axie Infinity. You can raise, trade, and combat 'Axies,' which are digital pets, on this NFT marketplace. Consider Pokémon, but this time it's online.

When executing any action, in-game tokens called AXS are utilized to trade, which can subsequently be traded for ETH and then swapped for traditional currency. The global active player base currently stands at 90,000 and is rising in tandem with the game's popularity. As a result, the most expensive Axie pet sold for $788,000 (Ong, 2021).

Tokens may also be gained by building kingdoms for these pets, so virtual real estate is also being sold here. The greatest trade possibility comes from simply playing the game and participating in the community. There is money to be made on this site, but it does not operate in the same way as other marketplaces.

In Chapter 4, I discussed virtual worlds and offered you some information about Decentraland. Buying and selling virtual real estate is extremely popular, particularly if the virtual real estate is located in Decentraland. This is the place to be, with digital artists purchasing real estate in order to display their work in virtual galleries. Sotheby's even has an art gallery there.

A block of land does cost thousands of dollars to purchase, but it is well worth the expense. The more parcels purchased, the more that can be done with the land, including renting it out.

As a result, virtual real estate, like traditional real estate, is an excellent investment option. It can be a little more complicated than other NFTs, so your best bet is to deal with a business called Public Realm, which was formed specifically for digital real estate investing. Regardless of the intricacy, it is well worth the effort, and the time has come to get in there and start buying!

SOCCER

Sorare is built on the fantasy football concept, with users collecting player cards to compete in weekly fantasy matches. The network is Ethereum-based and features licensed player data from over 140 soccer (European football) clubs in the United States, Europe, and Asia.

Cards include player data and rarity, with the most expensive card fetching $102,000. With over two billion soccer fans worldwide, the card was of Cristiano Ronaldo, and it is a very popular trading site.

MUSIC

BAND Royalty, a website that allows fans to obtain NFTs and then stake them to collect royalties, is well ahead of the competition. Instead of making money through NFT trading, you might make a nice passive income this way. To purchase this form of NFT, you only need to create an account and have ETH in your MetaMask wallet. Then you join the Music Mogul Club by purchasing one BAND NFT and begin staking!

The following is how staking works: Stakes receive an additional 5% off OpenSea Ethereum exchanges, effectively a discount. The NFTs are invested in the BAND Royalty pools, reducing supply in trading markets. This raises the value of the NFT, allowing you to gain more. Fans and users can also choose from three music pools: publishing, mechanical or public performance, and interest. Stakers can stake for periods ranging from 91 days to 5 years. The longer the stake, the greater the profit.

BAND Royalty obtains royalties directly from music industry leaders and splits them 50/50 with stakeholders. Revenue is collected when artists perform and their work is streamed and published in the BAND Royalty platform's music collection.

TWEETS

Tweets have become the thing to collect after the first one was auctioned for $2.9 million. The only NFT marketplace that sells tweets is Valuables. As long as you have ETH, you can sign up for an account and then copy and paste the URL of the tweet you wish to purchase into the search field.

The software will notify the sender of the tweet that someone wishes to purchase it, and the transaction will then take place. However, if it is a particularly popular tweet, there will be bidding. The winner is determined by the owner of the tweet. The winner will receive a minted NFT with the owner's signature. Anyone can utilize the site, and tweets range from unusual to common. It's becoming more popular, especially because almost everyone is on Twitter, so owning a famous tweet might be lucrative. In this digital age, it's akin to having that person's autograph.

This is a terrific area to trade if you check your Twitter account on a daily basis and know what is popular so you can make an offer.

At the time, there are three stumbling blocks:

- Even if the author does not accept your offer to purchase, you will still be charged the gas fees.

- You do not have ownership of the copyright.

- Even if you can resell the tweet, you must currently use OpenSea to do so.

NFT ART BUYING AND SELLING

If you have enough funds to invest in NFT art trading, you are currently guaranteed some good returns. Like physical art investing, you'll need a lot of money to get started, but you don't have to be a millionaire to get started. You only need enough to purchase cryptocurrencies for petrol and the art itself. It's impossible to give you an estimate of how much you'll need to get started because petrol prices fluctuate so often, and the same is true for purchasing digital art to sell. You would need to look at your budget and then calculate from there. Never begin with credit and constantly keep an eye on the market for trends.

Follow artists and crypto investors on social media platforms such as Twitter and Instagram since they are more likely to know what niche is becoming hot. Twitter is the most popular, so create an account if you don't already have one and begin following investors and artists discussing NFTs.

The goal is to get in early on this trend so that you can buy cheaply and sell as prices rise. Examine what kinds of artwork are already available, as well as what they were purchased for a few months ago and what their current value is. That should tell you that the market for that particular segment is currently saturated. If you have enough money to buy some high-end items, trade on Nifty Gateway, *OpenSea, SuperRare, Rarible, and Foundation. These marketplaces started it all and continue to maintain unique treasures that fetch high prices.*

They also have frequent drops, so if you're interested in trends and young artists, you may purchase a collection of theirs at one of these drops for a low price and then sell each piece at a good price.

You should also have multiple marketplace accounts so that you may diversify. Popular artists will typically sell their work at exorbitant prices, but they will also perform drops. These are excellent buys since you can get a collection of a well-known artist for a few hundred dollars and resell each piece at a premium price because the artist is well-known. Don't buy art on the secondary market since it's a gamble that could cost you a lot of money with no assurance of a return on investment.

Even though crypto art trading can result in a lot of money, there are so many different sorts of NFTs out there, and more are being invented all the time, that you should consider investing in these as well.

CHAPTER 8: THE STEP-BY-STEP GUIDE TO CREATING NFTS AND MAKING A PROFIT

With all of this information, I felt it would be best to summarize by setting down a very basic step-by-step method as a checklist for you to follow.

CREATING A NON-TRADABLE TRUST (NTT) TO SELL

1. Make a digital piece of art or scan a piece of actual art in high definition.

2. Construct a MetaMask wallet.

3. Purchase ETH.

4. Select a platform for the NFT marketplace.

5. Make an account on that platform.

6. Create an NFT by following the steps provided by the platform.

7. Pay the gas costs.

8. Put the NFT on the market.

9. Promote your artwork through social media or through friends and relatives.

10. Purchasing NFTs in Order to Sell

11. Construct a MetaMask wallet.

12. Put in some ETH.

13. Select a few high-end NFT marketplace systems.

14. To be notified of drops, create numerous accounts, and subscribe to their email lists.

15. Keep an eye on Twitter for emerging trends and niches.

16. Buy NFTs that are selling inexpensively in drops that are part of a collection based on that information.

17. Sell every piece in that collection on a secondary market within an hour after purchasing it.

18. If you follow these instructions, you will begin to notice earnings.

Here are a few things to keep an eye out for when you begin your journey into NFT trading. It's critical to keep these in mind and follow them if you want to get the most out of this experience.

TRENDS

The idea is to keep an eye out for patterns and to buy when prices are low. Twitter is the best source, but if you want to broaden your trading, join Discord discussions on upcoming technology and topics to obtain a deeper understanding. Most platforms include a link in their FAQs that allows you to sign up for and join Discord. It is a popular online communication tool for conversations.

SECOND-HAND MARKETS

Never buy from a secondary marketplace since you will pay more for NFTs and have a low probability of reselling for a profit. Because such marketplaces are where most people buy to collect, you should only sell on the secondary market.

FEES FOR GAS

Always be aware of gas expenses and keep enough ETH on hand to cover them. Make it a part of your purchasing budget so it doesn't come as a surprise after each mint or purchase.

PATIENCE

Even though NFT trading is a popular topic and many people have made money from it, it may take some time. Continue to follow the instructions outlined at the beginning of the chapter. The challenge is to buy and sell at the proper time, and only time will teach you what to look for.

Despite the fact that NFTs and marketplace platforms are minted and formed on the blockchain, you must be mindful of the hazards.

HOW TO KEEP YOURSELF SAFE AND SECURE

Using anything digitally and being online does not imply that it is secure. As a result, it's critical to keep yourself safe and secure at all times.

This chapter is not intended to scare you away from the internet, but rather to educate you on proper practices.

INTERNET SECURITY

Before using the internet, it is critical to have strong antivirus software. Depending on your budget, you have a variety of options to pick from. Please avoid using any that are free since they will not give proper security. Bitdefender, Kaspersky, Webroot, Norton, Trend Micro, McAfee, ESET, and Avast are among the finest.

AUTHENTICATION USING MULTIPLE FACTORS

When you log onto websites, this strategy protects you from being hacked. To gain access to these sites, you must give two or more pieces of information to prove that you are who you say you are. This is extremely important, and you can set it up with an app on your phone. You can select one of the five finest on the market: Authy, Google Authenticator, andOTP, LastPass Authenticator, and Microsoft Authenticator.

In March 2021, many Nifty Gateway users failed to employ multifactor authentication, resulting in collections being taken from their wallets and additional purchases being made using the cryptocurrencies in their virtual wallets. The organization was not hacked; rather, the users did not have adequate protection in place to protect their accounts.

SCAMS TO BE AWARE OF

There are several things to be aware of when undertaking NFT trading to avoid falling victim to a scam. Because NFTs are a new and popular technology, it stands to reason that the criminal element sees this as a fantastic opportunity to prey on those who are not secure and don't know what to look out for. Keep an eye out for safeguards and new developments as you hunt for trends to purchase and sell NFTs so that you can stay secure.

NFT DATA STORAGE

Some vendors keep their NFTs on centralized servers, despite the fact that not everyone follows standard practices. This could imply that if the server is broken or destroyed, the NFT will vanish. That is why it is critical to verify storage when purchasing to ensure that your NFT will remain operational. This is true for NFTs that you are collecting or hanging onto in order to sell later.

FAUX NFTS

Many marketplaces may list work that isn't the artist's work, so it's up to you to do the extra legwork to confirm you have the correct NFT and that it's being sold with the artist's consent. You can use a reverse-image search to discover whether it appears on other marketplaces but is labeled differently. Artists can list their work in many places, but they cannot change the name.

For example, two of the most popular markets, OpenSea and Rarible, do not need owner verification; as a buyer, you should be aware of this.

SITES OF PHISHING

With the advent of so many NFT marketplace platforms, with more appearing on a daily basis, it's vital to remember that not all are safe. There are phishing websites. These pose as genuine NFT marketplaces and steal user log-in credentials in order to steal collections for trade. These will appear to be reputable marketplaces, so do your homework before registering. Keep an eye out for giveaways, which are misspelled words on the website, such as 'cryptocurrency' being spelled as *'cryptokurrency,'* so keep an eye out for them.

This is when your multifactor authentication app comes in to protect you from losing your data and collection.

FRAUDULENT SUPPORT

Because there is a need for additional information about NFTs, scammers have set up customer support lines and social media pages to provide it. Be aware of any site that requests personal information from you since they will use it to gain access to your account. Obtaining information is one thing; exchanging it for personal information is a red flag.

GIVEAWAYS

Also, avoid clicking on any odd links. There are no freebies or drops requiring you to click on a link. If you receive any weird emails, such as those from a reputable website, do not click on them. Instead, use your browser to navigate directly to the site. If the email is genuine, the identical information can be accessed straight on the site. The same is true if you notice any pop-up giveaways on social media. Drops can sell for very little money, but never for free, which should be a big red flag that you're dealing with a scam.

TRADING IN WASHING MACHINES

There have been reports of NFT owners inflating the price by creating false buzz. Because they have a big amount of bitcoin in their virtual wallets, they are referred to as 'crypto whales.' They then sell an NFT from one wallet to another for more than it is worth. This is known as 'wash trading,' because the scammer owns both wallets.

APPS THAT IMPERSONATE VIRTUAL WALLETS

A user had downloaded what he thought was a virtual wallet called Trezor. He had lost all of his cryptocurrencies and was upset that the Apple Store carried phony software.

The truth is that it is simple to design apps that pass the majority of security checks. That is why internet security is critical. Even if the user took the time to compare the software to what the real thing looks like, he would still have a full virtual wallet.

Stick to well-known apps and virtual wallets, and always double-check the spelling and appearance of the app.

CHAPTER 10: THE PROS AND CONS OF NFTS

Because the information is extensive, I thought it could be useful to include a section on advantages and drawbacks so you have one handy when considering whether or not to begin trading. This is by no means meant to discourage you from taking advantage of the biggest thing in cryptocurrencies to date. This is simply to guarantee that you are fully prepared and informed before you begin trading. It is, in a sense, a final check to underline the reasons for wanting to be a part of something interesting and profitable, as well as a part of technological history.

CONS

UNPREDICTABILITY

Prices for collectibles are expensive and do not keep value over time, thus it is a gamble owing to the volatile nature of this form of trading. This is happening because it is so new and exciting that everyone, including investors, wants to be a part of it.

This is driving up prices, but despite the fact that NFTs can sell for a lot of money, prices have fallen. It is not always possible to make millions on a single piece.

The same can be said of any new and interesting artwork: everyone rushes in to be a part of it, and the popularity drives up the price. But it is not a bubble that will burst; rather, it is the beginning of a technology revolution and a new method to make money smartly and without a lot of hard labor.

SECURITY

NFTs can be stolen or lost if details are input improperly if passwords are not kept secure. Many artists' works have been tokenized without their consent, and it's unclear how to restore ownership at this point. The same cannot be said for frauds in the art sector. There have also been incidents of art provenance being tainted, which can have an impact on the historical accuracy of a work of art.

As this is an issue with other online payments, the safest solution is to follow the same principles for every internet transaction. It is not a new type of security risk; it is only being highlighted since everyone must follow the standards required to keep their information safe and secure so that they can use the internet safely.

PROS

BENEFIT FOR ARTISTS

Artists can collect royalties and be compensated for their work that cannot be reproduced, ensuring that artists are taken care of and knockoffs are not ubiquitous. As an NFT artist, this is not only a good way to ensure that your artwork gets noticed, but it is also a good way to earn money from each resale. It's making it easier to follow your passion and make a living from it.

INTRODUCING ART TO EVERYONE

Collectibles and art are more involved and entertaining, with a wide range of items to look at and appreciate. NFTs are making art acquisition and appreciation accessible to everyone. It's almost like an art and collectibles rebirth, with so many options and modern technology to choose from. It's exactly what the world needs now and in the future, and hopefully, it's here to stay.

AUTHENTICITY

Ownership is recorded in the ledger and confirmed against the item, ensuring that you receive a legitimate object that appreciates in value. Blockchain technology is integrated into the creation and use of NFTs, allowing transactions to be recorded on a ledger and traced. With each sale, ownership is recorded.

EASE

NFTs are simple to produce and sell since there are so many marketplaces to select from, each with a unique set of features and easy-to-follow step-by-step instructions. This simplifies the process of purchasing and selling crypto digital art.

Finally, trading NFTs is an excellent approach to get passive income. If you're a digital artist, you'll need to create something first before minting it into an NFT, but the return on investment will be sufficient to keep you from needing to sell work every day or week. Many people make thousands, if not millions, of dollars by just trading in NFTs. They acquire the correct piece inexpensively, just before it is going to trend, and then sell it for a higher price. All it takes is keeping an eye on the market for the correct trends.

I hope my book was able to provide you with insight into the NFT process as well as how to get started trading NFTs. It is a good passive income source, but it also requires planning and having the necessary information to make the right judgments.

With so many marketplaces to pick from for the many forms of trade accessible, anything can be purchased and sold as an NFT as long as you have some bitcoin in your virtual wallet, to begin with!

Begin today by creating your virtual wallet, purchasing ETH, and using Mintable by following the instructions to get a feel for the interface. You'll be trading like a pro in no time, making money on new and emerging NFTs or rare collectibles.

If you're a digital artist, you may imagine yourself receiving the acclaim you deserve, and your art may bring in enough money for you to finally be able to quit your day job and continue producing!

Finally, please keep in mind that I am not a financial counselor and am unable to provide financial advice. I am merely sharing information based on my own research.

I hope you found the material useful and that it inspires you to believe that this is the future of trade and that you are a part of history in the making.